TOPLESS MUM

Ron Hutchinson

TOPLESS MUM

OBERON BOOKS
LONDON

First published in 2008 by Oberon Books Ltd
521 Caledonian Road, London N7 9RH
Tel: 020 7607 3637 / Fax: 020 7607 3629
e-mail: info@oberonbooks.com
www.oberonbooks.com

A catalogue record for this book is available from the British Library.

ISBN: 978-1-84002-863-8

Cover photograph by Deejpilot (iStockphoto)

Characters

BARRY

ANNIE

TIFFANY

KYLE

KENNEDY

MITCH

The first London production of *Topless Mum* was performed at the Tricycle Theatre on 28 May 2008 with the following cast:

BARRY, Alistair Wilkinson
ANNIE, Emma Lowndes
TIFFANY, Louise Kempton
KYLE, Giles Fagan
KENNEDY, Sylvestra Le Touzel
MITCH, Jason Deer

Director Caroline Hunt
Design Conor Murphy
Music John O'Hara

It was originally co-produced by the Tobacco Factory Theatre and Imagineer productions and performed under the title *Topless Mum In Dead Hero Shocker!!!!* at the Tobacco Factory Theatre, Bristol on Wednesday 23 May 2007 with the following cast:

ANNIE, Maggie O'Brien
KYLE, Giles Fagan
GRACECHURCH (CHIEF EXECUTIVE), Peter Ellis
BARRY, Alistair Wilkinson
TIFFANY, Louise Kempton
MITCH, Jason Deer
KENNEDY, Bella Merlin

Director Caroline Hunt
Designer Ruth Hall
Digital Artist Nathan Hughes
Sound Design Elizabeth Purnell
Lighting Design Paul Towson
Stage Manager Rosamund Julie Davis
Costume Supervisor & ASM Jo Nicholls
Producer Dan Danson
Lighting design Mark Howland
Video design Jack Phelan

Topless Mum

In the blackout the screen shows a middle-aged woman smiling at the camera in front of a block of council flats –

BARRY: That's my mum –

The screen shows the crewcut, twenty-something BARRY standing grinning beside a car –

That's my car –

The screen shows a blurred image –

That's my thumb, silly bugger I am –

The screen shows BARRY kneeling by an Alsatian dog –

That's my dog, that's Prince, that is. Slavering Jaws of Death.

The screen shows four young men with short hair cuts, mugging for the camera. Three, including BARRY, are white; MITCH is black –

That's me and Dave and Paddy and Mitch. We'd had a forty-eight just before we shipped out. We got bladdered –

The screen shows another shot of BARRY posing with his dog –

That's me and Prince again –

The screen shows the aftermath of a car bombing; with severed limbs lying around the blackened chassis –

When a bomb goes off, you get this pressure wave, see, from the blast. It's very interesting. When it hits the body it goes inside you, like, it's got to go someplace so it exits at the weakest point, which is your joints. That's why you get all those arms and legs lying around after. You mightn't have a scratch on you but you can have all sorts missing. What a game, eh?

The screen shows BARRY at his car again as the lights rise and we see BARRY, on crutches with ANNIE, both watching the screen –

Me and my car again –

The screen shows a naked man in a hood. He's covered in blood and chained around the neck. A large German Shepherd is snapping at him, held by one of two British soldiers in uniform, backs to the camera.

It's in their culture, like, these, you might say, Eastern and Far Eastern people, that a man's a man. You've got to admire it in some ways. It might look like medieval shit to us – on their knees to Mecca and the women in bin liners wi' just their eyes showing – I mean, we are superior, aren't we, there's no question of that, our civilisation –

ANNIE: When somebody asked Gandhi what he thought of Western civilisation he said *What civilisation?*

BARRY: Well he were a cunt, weren't he?

ANNIE: You don't think there's anything they have that we don't?

BARRY: A lot more dead dogs in the street. A lot more kiddies with no shoes on their feet. You're one of them, are you?

He looks at her, hostile and the screen goes blank –

Is that what your game is?

ANNIE: I was just interested in your reaction to a place that must have been very different to anything you'd ever seen before.

BARRY: A shitheap's a shitheap, in't it? It don't make it any better that they're shooting at you.

He pauses –

I thought you lot tape-recorded all this stuff?

ANNIE: I'd like to do that if it's all right by you.

BARRY: Dunno. I suppose. Liberty Hall, here.

He shrugs and watches as she takes out a small tape recorder and turns it on.

ANNIE: You were saying how tough Afghanistan was –

BARRY wrong-foots her by grinning widely –

BARRY: It weren't so bad, love. It's what we trained for. Better than slogging through Bosnia with your bollocks frozen. That were a shitheap, too. Bloody great hills and Bosnians. When you come to look at it fairly, the whole bloody world is, in't it? Outside Bolton. And this ain't so hot either, is it?

He hesitates, looks at her with suspicion –

I don't know about this.

ANNIE: It's up to you. You came to us. If you're having second thoughts –

BARRY: Went to Belgium on a weekend once. Fat buggers, full of chips.

The screen shows one of the images of BARRY with his car again –

Sorry –

The screen shows one of the images of his dog –

Ooops –

The screen shows the image of the naked man again –

You want to break one of them down, you've got to humiliate him. Sarcasm does not work. They have this martyr complex, see? *Tie this brick of high explosive around my waist and blow myself into a million pieces? Okay, that sounds just the ticket. Ticket to Paradise. Ticket out of here. I'll have some of that.* Human life, I suppose, we have different values to the other races. So how do you fight it? Eh? I mean you don't see these fellas trailing behind their missuses at Asda. They wear the trousers. *Can I nip out for a quick half after I've done the dishes, pet?* is a phrase unheard of among them. So you go for his manhood, don't you? Psychological, see. The weak point. The point of attack. And it works. Can't argue wi' it. Worked in Iraq, Abu Ghraib, whatever it was called, it worked, don't let them tell you different.

ANNIE: You were in Iraq?

BARRY: First lot in, in Basra, before it all went to shite. Yesterday's news that, though, love. That's all put to bed.

ANNIE: But you were using the same tactic in Afghanistan? Breaking them down for interrogation?

BARRY is suddenly cagey –

BARRY: Is that what you want me to say?

ANNIE: I want to know the truth.

BARRY: Well you could say it were that –

ANNIE: Was it?

BARRY: Or you could say it were just a lark.

ANNIE: A lark?

BARRY: It were just a fragment of fun.

ANNIE: You really want me to write that?

BARRY: I don't care what you write, pet, I'm just telling you.

He gestures at the screen, shrugs –

It looks a lot worse than it were.

ANNIE: Our readers may find that hard to believe.

BARRY: They can believe what they like, pet.

ANNIE: You did take that photo, though?

BARRY: I might have done.

ANNIE: But you're saying you didn't have any responsibility for what it shows?

BARRY: Am I?

ANNIE: You were just the finger on the button?

BARRY: Was I?

ANNIE: Even so, you were *involved.*

BARRY: How's that, then?

Someone else enters. She's BARRY's wife, TIFFANY.

TIFFANY: Is she putting this on tape?

BARRY: I said it were all right.

TIFFANY: (*To ANNIE.*) On tape is it?

ANNIE: Do you mind?

TIFFANY: Dunno. Never done owt like this before. (*Shrugs.*) I suppose it's all right.

ANNIE: If we go ahead with this – if – a lot of questions are going to be asked about the exact nature of Barry's involvement.

BARRY: But I weren't involved. It were the camera.

ANNIE: It didn't go –

She mimes holding up a camera and pressing the button –

– by itself.

TIFFANY: You're a riot, you are.

ANNIE: You never thought to protest?

TIFFANY: Protest?

ANNIE: About the way these men were being treated?

TIFFANY: Which were nowt to do with him.

ANNIE: I want to make sure you know what you might be getting into. Put it like this. I'm a journalist. I often have a photographer with me on assignment. Say we're covering a demonstration. If somebody throws a brick at a policeman, he can take the photo. What I'm not allowed to do is put a brick in someone's hand and ask him to throw it, so that we can get the photo.

TIFFANY: But he ain't a reporter. And he don't work for a paper.

ANNIE: But the principle's the same.

TIFFANY: So fuck off, then. You know where the door is.

ANNIE keeps her temper –

ANNIE: When you pressed the button what kind of photo did you think you were taking? A record of something? A celebration?

BARRY: It were a souvenir.

The screen shows an old black and white photo of a second world war soldier in desert camo –

That's my grandad in the Second World War. Brought back a Jerry's helmet with a hole in it.

The screen shows a colour photo of a soldier standing below a Chinook helicopter –

That's me own dad in the Falklands. One of his mates cut off an Argie's ear with a razor and made a baccy pouch out of it. I just got a bunch of shrapnel up the arse.

TIFFANY: Only when he gets back he's thinking a photo like that might be worth a bob or two.

BARRY: You do pay for stuff like this, don't you?

ANNIE: Somebody tried something like this before. Sold *The Mirror* some fake photos.

TIFFANY: I heard about that. Yeah. Made right mugs of them, didn't they?

ANNIE: Right mugs.

TIFFANY: So are you saying, like – is that tape going, Barry? – you're accusing us, like? You're saying – (*To BARRY.*) – make sure the little red light's on – (*To ANNIE.*) – you're saying it's a con job?

ANNIE: There are good reasons for me to ask.

TIFFANY: Forget the whole thing. Stuff it. Give that here.

He holds a mobile phone out to her –

Soon as I saw it I said to him leave it alone. Delete the bloody thing. Have nowt to do with it.

She takes it from him –

I hate these things anyway. I were coming up the steps by the Co-op last week and my mate Trish says *I think that fella there is some kind of flasher only he's taking digis off his cell phone of your knickers, under your skirt* and he were and all, they'd been watching him from the Three Cooks and the police had him, it were in the paper, he were laid off from the wallpaper shop me mam broke her heel outside last year.

ANNIE: I wouldn't do that –

TIFFANY: Do what?

ANNIE: Delete it. Not yet. Not until I can get you an answer.

BARRY: (*To TIFFANY.*) Maybe you was right. See nowt. Hear owt. Say nowt.

TIFFANY: Bloody cow calls us liars to us faces –

ANNIE: You're going to have to give me the phone. I'll have the photo downloaded, then you can have it back. We need to check it out, validate it. Then we can talk about what we do.

TIFFANY looks irresolutely at BARRY –

TIFFANY: What do you think?

BARRY: Maybe you're right. It's too much of a hassle.

ANNIE: Don't – please –

She steps towards TIFFANY, involuntarily, eyes on the camera –

You've gone this far. I can't make any promises but let me see what could happen next.

TIFFANY shrugs and hands the phone back to BARRY –

TIFFANY: You sort it out.

BARRY holds out the phone for ANNIE –

BARRY: Make it quick love, eh? I've been buggered around enough since I got this –

He indicates his injured leg.

TIFFANY: That's got to be worth real dosh, in't it? Wouldn't you say?

Her mind made up, ANNIE's hand closes on the mobile –

But like he says, make it smartish, love. You're not the only paper out there. Me, I wouldn't wipe my backside with yours but Baz said ask you first.

BARRY: You're going to think this funny – but I won five hundred nicker off you in a scratcher game a couple of years back. It's like I owed you. And I like the sports.

TIFFANY: So how about it, then? He needs the dosh. Now he's out of the army and going into mobiles.

ANNIE: Mobiles?

BARRY: My cousin has a stall at the market. You wouldn't believe the money in it. It's all knocked-off, of course, back of a lorry stuff, fell off a container at Felixstowe, no questions asked but bloody hell, the gelt. Mobiles. It's the way to go, in't it? You'd have to say.

TIFFANY and BARRY exit, with BARRY walking on crutches. ANNIE remains on stage. The screen goes blank as ANNIE's editor KYLE enters. He takes the mobile from her –

KYLE: Have you walked into something recently and sustained a blow to the head? You know what happened to Piers Morgan. It's not a story – it's a suicide note.

ANNIE: I had it checked out by Pictorial. They printed it up, took a really close look at it – it doesn't seem to be a fake.

KYLE: I imagine *The Mirror* thought that.

ANNIE: I have Barry on the record.

KYLE: Lying through his teeth?

ANNIE: I think his wife started to get cold feet. Not because it's a fake. Because she was afraid of what they were really getting into. As if she'd never thought it through until then.

He proffers the mobile to her again but she shakes her head –

If it is the real thing? We'd be running it if *The Mirror* hadn't happened.

He flips the camera open, looks at the screen, as if wanting to test what he's saying by hearing the words aloud, as if musing –

KYLE: One could say, of course, that the real guts it would take to run this would be a tribute in itself to the reporter who got the story and – perhaps even more so – the editor who okayed it –

ANNIE: One could say that a good journalist can't be scared off a lead just because somebody else got their fingers burned –

KYLE tosses the mobile in his hand –

KYLE: You're sure they've taken it nowhere else?

ANNIE: I told you – they started fighting in front of me about whether they should be even doing it.

KYLE: They don't have an agent? A lawyer?

ANNIE: They're greedy but dumb.

KYLE: Ouch.

ANNIE: He had no idea what I was talking about when I suggested that taking a photograph of an atrocity might be in itself an atrocity.

KYLE: You don't think you're over-selling this? Scandal, yes, if properly handled – outrage, maybe – atrocity? Shouldn't we keep that for something – well – atrocious?

ANNIE: It's torture. Remember Abu Ghraib?

KYLE: Midfield for Chelsea?

ANNIE: Come on –

KYLE: That's yesterday's story.

ANNIE: This time the military can't write it off as a few bad apples.

KYLE: (*Warning.*) We're the paper which stands up for our boys, remember. Can't have good old Barry – Baz – labelled *Gestapo*.

ANNIE: Once in a while a story comes along – even here – that reminds you of why you wanted to be a journo. If it can be hung around a killer visual even better – and that's what we've got.

KYLE: A killer visual? A bunch of what our target reader – bless his heart – might see as one more bollock-naked wog getting what was coming to him? Nude women we like, yummy, yes. Nude men? We've not brought our core demographic that far along yet.

ANNIE: But men being brutalised by British soldiers.

KYLE: It would have to be a splash. The whole front page, a banner, three or four pages inside, an editorial. If we commit to it we have to commit full bore. We'd be in all the way up to our bollocks.

He takes out his Blackberry and texts a reply to something as he talks to her.

– And forget the Abu Ghraib angle. That's yesterday's chip wrapper. I don't give a flying fuck about that and you don't either, when it comes down to it. Much less the good old British public. But we *might* care that the British Tommy is being made to fight an endless dirty war that's getting muck on his hands and by extension ours not to mention them sending Prince Harry over there for a couple of hours playing Silly Buggers though unfortunately they brought him out before he could stop a rocket up the arse which would have been a story and a half. That just might be an angle for us.

ANNIE: And this paper is the only one with the guts to go for it, after *The Mirror* debacle?

Sensing that he's coming round to her point of view –

The British soldier is the salt of the earth, of course but he's being made to do things that we should be ashamed of. Or maybe not. Maybe we do need to have these things done, however gruesome and unpleasant, to keep us safe. Maybe that's a case worth arguing but it should be argued in the open, with all the evidence in. (*Exasperated at his Blackberrying.*) Could you keep your bloody thumbs still for a moment? (*Passionately.*) This is a great story. Okay, it's not *Soap Star Found in Love Nest* –

KYLE: We do *Soap Star in Love Nest* really really well.

ANNIE: But we didn't sign up to track Soap Stars to their Love Nests, did we?

KYLE: I need to tug the lip about this one. I'll get back to you. Meantime take your pick – Soccer Star's Kinky Threesomes, Pop Star's Sex Bombshell or My Torrid Nights of Love With Supermodel?

ANNIE: I'll take the supermodel. It sounds by far the most nationally important of the three.

KYLE: That's irony, cutie. We don't do irony. It doesn't come off the page well.

ANNIE: But in real life? Just between you and me?

KYLE: There is no real life. We are figments of the Owner's dream world. All this is an illusion. Isn't it too preposterous to be real?

ANNIE: Preposterous or sad?

KYLE: We don't do sad either. It doesn't sell papers.

ANNIE: But again – between you and me? If we were being honest?

KYLE: Spell that?

ANNIE: Honesty between two people?

KYLE: I can't find it sad, no. Because that would make me, who spends his life at this desk, ridiculous for staying here. I'd hate for you to think me that.

ANNIE: Trapped, then? By the salary, the perks, the wife and kids?

He turns abruptly away from her –

KYLE: Wouldn't have a picture of him with his missus, would you? Just in case we run it?

ANNIE: As a matter of fact –

She takes out a small framed photo –

ANNIE: On the way out this photograph of Barry and his wife fell off the shelf into my handbag.

She hands it to him.

KYLE: My goodness – I did teach you well, didn't I?

ANNIE exits with KYLE as the screen shows the image of the naked prisoner again. We hear testimony being read in a flat, expressionless voice in an English accent –

KENNEDY: First they put the dogs on me. They hit me here and here. Then they said they would do sex with me. They would make me do sex with men. Then one of them said I would do sex with the dog first. I beg them not to take my clothes off but they say take everything off or you will be bitten by the dog again. It is great shame for me to be seen by somebody without my clothes, even my family. It is greater shame to be seen by a woman. I am crying, please do not do this, I will tell you what you want, anything you want but they bring a woman to look at me. She looks between my legs and says something and they laugh. The British soldiers laugh.

The lights rise on KENNEDY. She's a military lawyer, is wearing a British army uniform as she dryly reads the statement. Sitting facing her is MITCH, in military uniform, also.

I see other men. Men from my village. Old men, young men. We cannot look each other in the face. I see my brother. They know he is my brother. He is naked, too. We are all naked and the soldiers are laughing and the women soldiers say things about us. They tell us to touch each other. Below. If we do not do that they hit us and kick us and threaten us with the dogs again. We do those things. More soldiers keep arriving. One of them suggests one thing and someone else something else. That we have to do to each other. They make me and my own brother do a thing. Touching each other. I see his eyes when we are doing it. He looks dead. As if something has died in him.

MITCH lifts a hand over his mouth to suppress a yawn.

I'm sorry, am I boring you?

MITCH: It's just it's a bit hot in here, like.

KENNEDY: (*Icily.*) Try to bear with me.

She reads from the statement again –

They say we have taken photographs of you, touching each other. We will show them to your family, to your village. Even if we let you go, they will know what you did here. Your wives will know, your mothers, your sisters. The men in your village will know. We will tell them you were happy to do these things. It would be better to kill myself.

She slides the statement into a file, looks at MITCH –

Not good is it? Not good at all. For you.

MITCH: In what way, like?

KENNEDY: Victim says he was abused in British military custody on or around the time that photograph was –

She mimes taking a photo –

We know who took it. You were one of his oppoes. Fill in the gaps.

MITCH: It's about that photo, is it?

KENNEDY: Why else did you think you were here? To have a Mars bar with me?

MITCH: The one that's been in the papers?

KENNEDY: The one your mate took and sold to them.

MITCH: And this fella says it were him? On there?

KENNEDY: I've just been reading you his statement. Hallo?

MITCH: That that's him?

KENNEDY: That's what he claims and his dates add up.

MITCH: And he gave you a statement, like?

KENNEDY: You're starting to get the hang of this. Yes, he gave me a statement. I'm a lawyer but I'm also a soldier. The men who did this to that man aren't soldiers. Not by my definition. It's my job to find them and punish them. Now what might be in it for you?

Gathering all his powers of concentration, MITCH tries to work it out –

MITCH: So what you're saying is there's a photo, right, and he says he's on it even though he isn't on it but he says he is and Barry took it and it's summat to do wi' me only it were

Barry that took it, only he didn't, not if he's supposed to be on there, the fella that gave you the statement?

KENNEDY: That was very neatly put but my concentration must have wandered –

MITCH: There's a photo and he says he's on it even though he isn't on it but he says he is and Barry took it and it's summat to do wi' me only it were Barry that took it, only he didn't, is that it?

KENNEDY: I'd need a corkscrew to write that down. Is that the idea? You're going to keep denying it? Try to tie it in knots? That's what you agreed on with him?

MITCH: With who?

KENNEDY: Your mucker Barry.

MITCH: He's not my mucker.

KENNEDY: You do understand how serious this is? I am getting that across? As we're sitting here, having a little chinwag before we have to start thinking about things like cautions and close arrest.

MITCH: I'm just trying to get me head around it.

He makes another effort to understand –

MITCH: There's a photo that he isn't in –

KENNEDY: Which he may be in.

MITCH: But he's not –

KENNEDY: Please –

MITCH: But he says he is –

KENNEDY: Yes –

MITCH: Having the dogs put on him and that

KENNEDY: This is good, keep going –

MITCH: All that kinky sex stuff –

KENNEDY: I'm liking it –

MITCH: That stuff about his brother or summat –

KENNEDY: All part of the sexual humiliation he underwent –

MITCH: But he didn't. Or it would be on there, wouldn't it? But it can't be because it isn't him.

KENNEDY: It's like pulling teeth, this is –

MITCH: I'm trying to help, I am. I just can't get me head around it.

MITCH: I mean, who did what and why he's saying that.

KENNEDY: Because it happened? For starters? And unluckily for you and Barry there's a documentary record that nobody can argue with?

Smile – She mimes taking a photo again.

He did a bit of all right for himself, did Barry, out of this. How much do you think they paid for it? Enough for a new car? Two weeks in Benidorm? How'd you do? The price of a pint and a possible court martial, a dishonourable discharge?

MITCH: But I didn't do nowt.

KENNEDY: (*Ignoring it.*) You know what Barry is? He's a lad. He's got his head screwed on. Barry's in clover. But you – well – where are you in all this? Might be worth thinking about, mightn't it? Have a pull on that, pal. Dismiss and think on. The glasshouse beckons. I see a concrete bunk in your future, I really do.

The lights fade on him and he exits. ANNIE enters, faces KENNEDY –

Liked the law, didn't want to spend my life drawing up conveyances; had a quick look at the corporate world, liked that even less. Took a short service commission, travelled, skied, dived, liked that side of it. Always read a lot of history, got interested in military law – how people have tried to humanise the, I suppose, inhuman; liked the paradox, how to impose a legal framework on something that seems to have no rules; ended up here with no regrets, none. A happy warrior. Trying to puzzle her way through – well, you know. This mess.

Beat –

Must have taken a bit of courage, running this story after *The Mirror* balls-up.

ANNIE: I think there's a feeling that you rather got away with it last time.

KENNEDY: Round Two, this, is it? Second leg? Defending the honour of the British press? Now there's a concept.

Before ANNIE can respond –

You must have been in a bit of a rush. Would that be fair to say? Get the story out before another paper or the TV got hold of it?

ANNIE: The *truth* out, don't you mean?

KENNEDY: Oh come now – they're not called newspaper *truths* are they? Don't you call it *getting the story*?

ANNIE: This is a story of young men, whose lives have been destroyed by what you represent; both as a lawyer and a soldier – and maybe I'm thick but I still don't see how you can reconcile those two things, no matter how good the skiing is. Barry's on crutches. He's crippled for life. The man he helped abuse has had even more damage done to him, mentally and physically. I can't see that I have to feel embarrassed at arguing his case.

KENNEDY: You're not arguing his case. You're using him to sell newspapers – and to settle scores with us about *The Mirror*.

ANNIE: I don't work for *The Mirror*.

KENNEDY: But you all got a black eye. We won, for once. You're not used to that.

ANNIE: You think it's personal?

KENNEDY: It is for me. Something like this – if it's true – offends me at a deeper level than you could possibly understand. I'd be the one arguing the case and arguing it where it matters – in a court martial, where careers and people's freedom would be on the line.

ANNIE: *If* it's true?

KENNEDY: You can't send someone to die without a code of honour. A code of honour doesn't work without a sense of shame. And I had never been more ashamed than when I saw that photo.

ANNIE: Then for God's sake why not respond as a human being and not a uniform?

KENNEDY: Three hours ago I got the digital forensics back. It's a new field and a little over my head but basically they can look at the image and tell you if anyone has been manipulating it or if it's not exactly what it claims to be –

On the screen appears the photo of the abuse. She takes out a laser pointer and directs it towards it –

For example, what seems to be a bruise on this man's upper shoulder is actually this –

On the screen we see a magnified image which shows part of a tattoo –

The tattoo reads *Millwall Forever*. It's possible, of course, that Al Qaeda has decided to add some real muscle to global jihad but on the face of it, it seems improbable.

The laser beam indicates another part of the image –

The abuse seems to be taking place in a shipping container, which it's true, we do use for emergency housing in Afghanistan and yes, the man I interviewed said that's where he'd been interrogated. But when we blow up the serial number of the container –

On the screen we see a magnified image which shows a serial number –

We were able to track it with the International Shipping Registry and confirm that it's never been out of Europe. It was last used, in fact, to ship equipment from a British military base in Germany back to the United Kingdom for refurbishment. Currently it's here –

On the screen we see a container stacked with a pile of others in a British field –

Number Five Stores Depot, Kidlington. That's Kidlington, Oxfordshire. Not Kidlington, Helmand Province.

She snaps the pointer off –

Oh bad luck. Or was it carelessness? Or just rush?

She slides an envelope across the desk to the shocked ANNIE –

That's a copy of the report. Very technical. Could give you a headache. Hire your own people, Argue with it. But I'd say it rather looks like two-nil to us.

She exits and ANNIE turns to face the shocked KYLE as the screen goes blank –

KYLE: Holy mother of God. Sacred heart of Jesus. Shit shit shit shit shit shit shit. Millwall?

ANNIE: It looks like it.

KYLE: A field in Kidlington?

ANNIE: It seems so.

KYLE: Where Barry – fucking Barry – was last based?

ANNIE: Yes.

KYLE: No. You mean no, right? You checked it out, had the thing looked at by our experts, they said bollocks? They stood by our version, said this was a crude attempt by the military to derail our story?

ANNIE: Millwall. Kidlington.

KYLE: Lamb of God protect me now and at the hour of my death.

Remembering something –

His mobile? *He took it on his mobile?* What is he doing with a mobile in the middle of Afghanistan? Didn't anybody stop to ask that?

He sinks into the chair behind his desk, crushed –

Is this the *Beano*? Or is it a national bloody newspaper with a circulation of –?

He tails off, then snatches at a straw –

Wait a minute. The tape –

BARRY enters to reprise the contents of the tape with ANNIE –

ANNIE: *You were using the same tactic in Afghanistan? Breaking them down for interrogation?*

BARRY: *Is that what you want me to say?*

ANNIE: *I want to know the truth.*

BARRY: *Well you could say it were that –*

ANNIE: *Was it?*

BARRY: *Or you could say it were just a lark.*

ANNIE: *A lark?*

BARRY: *It were just a fragment of fun.*

ANNIE: *You really want me to write that?*

BARRY: *I don't care what you write, pet, I'm just telling you. It looks a lot worse than it were.*

ANNIE: *Our readers may find that hard to believe.*

BARRY: *They can believe what they like, pet.*

ANNIE: *You did take that photo, though?*

BARRY: *I might have done.*

ANNIE: *But you're saying you didn't have any responsibility for what was going on?*

BARRY: *Am I?*

ANNIE: *You were just the finger on the button?*

BARRY: *Was I?*

ANNIE: *Even so, you were involved.*

BARRY: *How's that, then?*

KYLE reacts as BARRY exits –

KYLE: So he never at any time told you in so many words that on a specific day at a specific time he took a photograph of specific Afghanis being brutalised?

ANNIE: He said he'd come back from Afghanistan and he had a photo.

KYLE: Which he did. Leaving you to fill in the gaps. Making two and two add up to five.

ANNIE: Anybody in the position I was in –

KYLE: Would have heard what he wanted you to hear?

ANNIE: Okay, so I didn't sit down with a transcript like a lawyer and look for the gaps in what he was saying –

KYLE: All he had to do was choose his words carefully. Or rather, the gaps in between them – into which you fell, arse over tit and yes, I am aware those words are outlawed by our sexual harassment policy –

ANNIE: (*Disbelieving.*) He couldn't have tricked me, he couldn't.

KYLE: Because he was wearing a shell suit and he breathes through his mouth? Because you thought you had their number the minute you saw them?

He gives a bitter grin –

Looking on the bright side, things are looking up if that's our average reader. Maybe there's more going on with them up top than we're giving them credit for.

ANNIE: Wouldn't you have gone for his story, too?

KYLE: I did. Remember? You dropped me in it alongside you.

ANNIE: You smelled something there.

KYLE: Not, unfortunately, the steaming yak turd that it turns out to be.

Tightly –

It just goes to show you what happens when you let principle get in the way of self-interest.

ANNIE: I don't think it was entirely principle, was it? You did spend the night at my apartment after saying yes.

Making sure he gets the message –

I know we make all that sexual harassment stuff a bit of a joke – working here, how could it be anything else? – but I really wouldn't like you to get the idea that I'm going to walk the plank on this one alone.

As ANNIE exits, TIFFANY enters, hostile and defiant –

TIFFANY: I wouldn't stand there if I were you, pet. Bloody dog did his business there. I think I got it all up but you never know with shag pile, do you?

Off balance, KYLE moves slightly to one side.

KYLE: The question is, what are we going to do about this?

TIFFANY: I told you, I don't know what you're talking about.

KYLE: The photo.

TIFFANY: You keep saying *the photo* but it's just banging your gums, to me.

KYLE: The photo wasn't real.

TIFFANY: It was a real photo, of real people. Not the Muppets. Are you saying it weren't?

KYLE: You implied it had been taken in Afghanistan.

TIFFANY: Imply-what?

KYLE: That Barry had taken it there.

TIFFANY: What? On his mobile? I don't think they get service there, do they? Hard enough to get it around here.

She puts an imaginary phone to her ear –

Can you hear me now? Can you hear me?

KYLE: My reporter was told he'd just come back.

TIFFANY: Oh, that stuck-up bitch. So he had.

Her mouth opens wide in mock surprise –

You thought he'd taken it there, did you? I don't think we ever said that.

She shakes her head –

You can check, if you like. Wasn't there one of them – what do you call them – a tape recorder?

KYLE: There was, yes.

TIFFANY: I thought there was. Then that'll tell you, won't it?

KYLE: Tell us that you laid a very careful trap for us?

TIFFANY: A trap, pet? I suppose you need a real imagination to work for the papers, do you?

KYLE: I'm full of admiration for you, believe me. I've tied people in knots over the years with words – words said, words not said – this was as expert a carving-up as I've ever seen. Congratulations.

TIFFANY: On what?

Her eyes are wide open in innocence –

We said Barry had just come back from Afghanistan –

KYLE: And he had a photo we might like to see, yes.

TIFFANY: If it all took on a life of its own after that – what's that to do wi' us? I think I told the girl we don't even read your bloody rag. In fact, I'm sure I said it. It'll be on the tape someplace.

KYLE: (*Grimly.*) I'm sure it will.

TIFFANY: So how was we to know? If you'd jumped to
confusions? Funny what folk say and what folk hear, in't it?
Like I'll say to Barry sometimes *You what?* and he'll say *You
what?* and neither of us'll have a clue what we're fighting
about only like me mam used to say there's listening and
there's hearing and they're not the same thing, usually
with a clip around the ear but I suppose she wanted to
hear what she heard, that reporter and you know what, it's
a funny thing but there was this picture of Barry and me,
I got the frame at Woolworths, but we must have looked
high and low and just can't put us hands on it. Wouldn't
happen to know anything about that, would you? Round
about the time she was here?

KYLE decides to take the gloves off –

KYLE: We're prepared to take whatever legal steps we have to
unless we can come to some kind of understanding; you,
me, your husband.

TIFFANY: How would that be, then?

KYLE: At the minimum we'd need a statement saying it was a
joke that got out of hand.

He takes a sheet of paper out –

I had our legal department draw something up.

TIFFANY: I don't know if we should sign that.

KYLE: I think you should.

TIFFANY: See me mam signed something for my cousin Billy
and when he got sent down they took her washing machine
and drier because he hadn't kept up the payments. Then
they went after her telly. She had all kinds of trouble.
Couldn't answer the bloody door wi'out somebody waving

a piece of paper at her and she'd just had a hysterectomy and all –

Beat –

Of course if we sign it'd be like an apology, wouldn't it, which'd mean we're saying we did summat wrong and as I don't know what you're talking about you'd better get your arse out of that door before I set Prince on you.

KYLE: I really wouldn't threaten me.

TIFFANY: That your motor out there, is it?

She peers past him, through the window –

The kids round here, they don't appreciate nowt. A nice car like that, it's like a magnet. How much'd a new paint job and windows cost? Out of interest?

KYLE's trying to keep his temper –

KYLE: I'm sure we can come to some agreement. I'm aware it might take another payment to do that.

TIFFANY: Hang on a minute –

She takes out a small tape recorder –

Could you say that again?

KYLE: You've been recording this?

TIFFANY: I thought I'd save you the bother.

Holding it out towards him –

Isn't that what you do? To make sure there's no argy-bargy? You want to say it again? The thing about more money?

KYLE chooses his words carefully –

KYLE: I'm not offering you more money. My only interest is in clearing this up.

TIFFANY: I wouldn't want you to go upsetting him. Not Barry. Could be dangerous, that. When he got blown up, see, the bang – well your head, inside, your brain, it's just like a big bowl of jelly or summat apparently. Summat got broken, like, in there, he come a bit unglued, you might say and I'm not saying he's not responsible for his actions but he's different since he came back. I mean *different.* I mean not just *hurt.* Different. So whatever she asked him about the photo and where it came from, whatever he might have said about it – be hard to put the blame on him, wouldn't it? Barry take you for a ride? Our Barry? The state he's in? I don't think so.

Unseen by KYLE, BARRY enters, listening, leaning on his crutches –

(*Innocently.*) I mean, didn't somebody – wasn't there summat about *The Mirror?* And a photo? Some time back?

KYLE: So what do you want? *You?* How do we put right this – clearly a – misunderstanding? You and me?

Before she can answer BARRY heads between them –

BARRY: I know what you thought you had, mate. Summat to have a go at the lads. Didn't you?

KYLE: We're the paper that supports our boys. We just wonder sometimes at what you're being asked to do. The price people like you have to pay.

BARRY: If this really was a war and we was fighting it for real, you ought to be hung, you lot. They ought put you in the Tower of London and hang you.

KYLE: (*Stung.*) I'm not a mug, Barry. Who are we trying to kid? There's a wonderfully old-fashioned-sounding legal phrase –*taking money under false pretences.* Ever come across it? Could it remotely possibly apply here? What do you think?

TIFFANY: Only if he said he were giving you summat and he gave you summat else.

KYLE: The bullshit aside we all know that's what you did.

BARRY: I don't know what she thought she was buying. I know what we was selling. In't that right, Tiffs?

KYLE: Do you have a lawyer? A good one? What happened to your mam because of cousin Billy's nothing to what we're going to do to you, unless we can get this cleared up.

TIFFANY: Hang on while I check if this is still going –

She makes a show of holding the tape recorder to her ear –

Yeah, all right, *proceed* –

KYLE tries to control his reaction –

KYLE: I know the sacrifices we ask you to make. I know how lousy a deal you've had. I can see that might affect your judgement so let's go with this statement –

TIFFANY: I'll give you a statement. You ready? It's a bloody good job he had a five-day leave before he shipped out because that's when I got up the spout with Brittany –

BARRY: Leave it –

TIFFANY: You had your say, I'm having mine –

BARRY: No –

TIFFANY: There ain't going to be any more little Brittanys –

BARRY: Don't –

TIFFANY: Or any more little Barrys or Jasons or Tiffanys – there ain't going to be any more of anything because he got his bollocks shot off, didn't he? It weren't just his head. What he came back without. He ain't a man, no more. Not a real man. That's how he sees it. I tell him he is to me, just not in that way –

BARRY: *Tiffs* –

TIFFANY: But he can't live wi' it. I'm managing. Just. But he's twenty-three and he's never going to do that no more. Never. With nobody. He can't even do it to himself. There's your bloody statement and you can stick it up your arse.

BARRY: That's private, that is. That's – that's – it's nowt to do wi' it, it's –

His fist is raised as if he's ready to beat her, despite the presence of KYLE –

You cow. You sodding cow. It were going to be easy, you said. You said it were easy money –

TIFFANY: Shurrup, you.

BARRY swings round at KYLE –

BARRY: It were her idea. Not mine. She said *The Mirror.* She said that were it. She said nobody'd think we'd be daft enough to try it on twice.

KYLE: Smashing. (*To TIFFANY.*) That tape still running, love?

TIFFANY: No it's not. And I told you – he's a head short of a full pint as well as missing his bollocks.

BARRY: Will you stop it? Will you fucking stop it?

TIFFANY: He don't know which way is up, half the time.

BARRY: (*To KYLE.*) I got blown up, see – I got – me head and – it were a convoy–routine – running stuff up to one of the sangars further up the Valley in Apache Country – only we hit this mine, see and I'm like a fucking rabbit out of the hatch because we're a sitting target for an RPG round now the treads have come off only I step on this mine, see, because it's all gone to fuck, we're being mortared, machine gunned, the whole bloody lot and for what, eh? What's it all been about? When they got a grip, when they unfucked it, when the chopper comes in for me I see the carrier on its side, the tracks off, and bog paper – yards of it – hundreds of yards of it – blowing all over the fucking desert. That's what'd been in the carrier – miles of bloody bog roll wrapped around every fucking rock as far as you could see.

TIFFANY turns to KYLE –

TIFFANY: Is that your motor down there, mate? Look what the little buggers have done to it –

As KYLE stares out of the window in shock the lights fade on BARRY and TIFFANY as they exit, rising on ANNIE as she enters, holding an envelope –

ANNIE: How bad is it?

KYLE: New wing mirrors, new paint job, twisted the bloody aerial right off.

ANNIE: What?

KYLE: My Saab.

ANNIE: I wasn't referring to that.

KYLE: It's three months old.

ANNIE: You told them we'd sue?

KYLE: Bit of a problem there. Barry seems to have some kind of head injury. Wouldn't look too good to drag a wounded war hero through the courts. In the heat of debate, one might say, the exact nature of his other injuries came out. Putting it delicately, he'll be singing soprano from now on.

ANNIE: He lost his –?

KYLE: Everything.

ANNIE: The? – and the? –

KYLE: Both – or all three, however you count them.

ANNIE: Poor bastard.

KYLE: My initial reaction, too.

ANNIE: They're all missing?

KYLE: I didn't carry out a personal inspection but I've no reason to believe they were lying.

ANNIE: You wouldn't about something like that, would you?

ANNIE hands him the envelope –

Take a look at these –

As he opens the envelope on the screen we see glamour shots of the younger TIFFANY –

I was wondering why she said she wouldn't wipe her backside with us. Could it be personal? Indeed it could. Pictorial had them. A few years ago she sent in a set of topless photos.

On the screen we see photos of a topless TIFFANY from ten years back –

It was a series about Army Wives. The idea was to remind our boys in Bosnia – remember Bosnia? – and we're the paper that supports our boys, remember – of what was waiting for them back home. They never used them. That could be why they approached us and not the *Mail* or anybody else. A grudge.

KYLE: What do I say except I'd give her one myself?

He shrugs –

Where does that get us?

ANNIE: I'm just thinking aloud here but does *Army Wife In Sex Pics Shocker*? *Topless Secrets Shame of Disabled Vet?*

KYLE: I applaud your instinctive recourse to blackmail, it shows a high degree of professionalism but –

ANNIE: We're still screwed?

KYLE: In a way that Tiffany never will be again. Or not by her old man, anyway.

KYLE hesitates –

On the other hand I had a lot of time to think on the way back down on the M6 – one sympathises with him and poor old Tiffany, of course. One can see that such a traumatising event would make one look around for a way to protest the military machine, the politicians who keep sending young men into harm's way.

ANNIE: That doesn't sound like them.

KYLE: Follow me carefully. Watch the bouncing ball. We know their real reason was to get into mobiles. But on the way back I'm thinking – as well as how much it's going to cost to get the Saab fixed – what might have been their unconscious motivation? Isn't it possible that they could all along have been trying to protest, in the only way they could, about the sacrifice they had to make? That it wasn't just an attempt to get their hands on the loot?

ANNIE: But that's what it was.

KYLE: Or was it *Heroes Afghan Nightmare – Underdog Fights Back*? You see where I'm going? Could one say that *Crippled war hero Barry Grove and his attractive young wife fought back*

tears as they told me the amazing truth behind the sensational
headlines? Could it have been that struggling to find the words,
they outlined a battle plan that would take even more courage
than the crippled heroes epic story of endurance in Afghanistan?

ANNIE: Does he have an epic story of endurance?

KYLE: He was blown up carrying a load of toilet paper and
then stepped on a land mine. But we can make it look as
if he was due a bloody Victoria Cross if we have to. Might
it not have been that *They would single-handedly take on the*
war machine of the British government and the entire might of the
military?

ANNIE: No, it mightn't. Did *you* walk into a door?

KYLE: I seem to remember your resumé said something about
a Creative Writing class at East Anglia. It's not showing.
Thinking aloud, let's say, yes, they faked the photo. But
not for money. They remembered how Abu Ghraib nearly
derailed Blair in Iraq, hammered the first real nail in his
coffin. They wanted to do the same thing for the boys in
Afghanistan and came up with a way to do that that was at
the same time an almost post-modern critique of the role
of the popular press in the way it used what happened at
The Mirror.

ANNIE: Post-modern –?

KYLE: Maybe that's taking it a little too far, yes – but can you
see the sliver of daylight that I can? What we'd have –
potentially – providentially – wouldn't be just a con-man
and his horrible wife but a bona fide hero. We'd have a
man with a conscience and the guts to do something about
it. Yes, we were taken advantage of, yes, one might say we
were an unwilling party to Barry's shenanigans –

ANNIE: But let's not judge the young couple until you've been
in their shoes?

KYLE: Or in Barry's underpants, in this case.

ANNIE: God forbid.

KYLE: It's a bit of a stretch but if it takes channelling your creative writer to get yourself out of this, you may want to try. Better that than a life of regret, I'd say, filing copy for the *Bridlington Weekly Advertiser and Fish Frier*.

ANNIE: Get *myself* out of it?

KYLE: You brought the story in, sweetie. I'd rather say it's up to you to fix it. (*Warning.*) A straight cash offer would dump us even deeper into the faecal matter but those photos now –

He looks up at the photos of the younger, nude TIFFANY –

– Tiffany's urge, like that of so many blushing English roses to get her kit off for the masturbating millions – possibly there's something there for us, if handled carefully, don't you think…?

The lights fade on KYLE who exits as a wary TIFFANY enters, gives ANNIE a hostile stare, under the nude photo –

TIFFANY: It were me Uncle took them. Think that's creepy, do you?

ANNIE: Did I say that?

TIFFANY: He were mad keen for his camera, he were. Welder but he thought he were some kind of – I don't know – photographer or summat. Had to keep it from me mam, she'd have killed him; right old fashioned she were. I don't think me dad ever saw her outside of her nightie in all the years they was married. My mates said he were only a dirty old man and he'd try to cop a feel at the very least of it but it weren't like that at all. Very respectful, he was. Felt a bit odd, of course, getting your kit off for a geezer three times your age, related to you, where he called his studio but it were just the spare room with all his gear in it. Bit sad, really. Never laid a finger on me. He'd done this course at the Technical College, 'The Nude', so he seemed to know his stuff. It weren't just *get them off* and a couple of snaps. He had lights and things, spent a lot of time setting it up. I were bloody freezing he took so long, *get a move on*, I thought but it had to be just right. (*Warning.*) I'm admitting nowt, though. And you ain't got nowt.

Deflecting the hostility, ANNIE looks up at the photo –

ANNIE: Saw something in you, did he? Was that it? Something special?

TIFFANY: I could have been a model, he said. I could have done it for a living. Not just topless. Clothes. Modelling. Said I had great hands. Said there are people make a living just modelling their hands or their legs or their hair or their smile. Like he says sometimes in the films that in't the movie star you're watching, it's somebody who looks like them from the back or the side. Makes you wonder what's what, don't it? How you'd know?

Looking up at the photo –

I never saw myself as that special. Nobody does really, do they?

ANNIE: I'm sure some people are convinced of it. I deal with them every day.

TIFFANY: Yeah well, your job, the people you meet – I'm talking about people on the bus, in the launderette, the ones *I* meet.

ANNIE: I think she was a very special person to have the courage to do what she did.

TIFFANY: (*Embarrassed.*) Knickers.

ANNIE: And if you only knew the ructions that photo on the mobile has caused –

TIFFANY: (*Defensive.*) I'm saying nowt about nowt about that, I told you. (*Suspicious.*) So how would it work, then? If it were like that? Like what you said? His protest?

ANNIE: You realise I'm just floating an idea, thinking aloud.

TIFFANY: Think all you bloody like. How'd it work?

ANNIE: You'd leave everything to us.

TIFFANY: (*Sharply.*) No I don't think so. I've always been able to think on me feet, I have, not like Barry, I mean even before he got that bang on the head he weren't the sharpest knife in the drawer, if you know what I mean. We'd be in the clear, like?

Hastily.

Which is not giving anything away; not that we did nowt wrong.

ANNIE: Of course not, but you must want it over and done with; the questions, the suspicion – the legal action that some people at the paper are still threatening –

TIFFANY: Which is why you can't pay nowt? Or not directly, like? Is that right? Just so I'm following this?

ANNIE: It wouldn't look good, you can see that.

TIFFANY: I don't know –

She pulls back and ANNIE tries to control her reaction as she sees any deal slipping away –

I mean, it weren't a protest, were it? Not about Afghanistan. Not about the Army. He loved the life. Loved everything about it. Protest? He'd have re-upped if he

hadn't got his bollocks blown off and his head done in.
Protest? So there's your first problem.

ANNIE: But his head *was* done in, wasn't it? So – and I'm
talking to you directly here, just you and me – so what
does it really matter what Barry has to say one way or the
other?

Risking everything, ANNIE shows her steel –

Who – to put it crudely – can make any sense of anything
he says? That's the thing about head injuries, I should
think – how can you know what's going on in there and
trust anything anybody who has had one comes out with?

Not giving the angry TIFFANY time to respond –

I know you're married to him, love, and you've stuck with
him but nobody really gives a flying fuck if Barry says
one thing today and something opposite tomorrow. That's
the beauty of it. Barry can be Barry without doing us any
damage because he's not quite right up here, is he? Like
you say, he may not have been the sharpest knife in the
drawer going into this but now?

She indicates her head –

I'm going straight to the point, you see and not round
and round in circles because my job's on the line and I
mean to keep it no matter who gets in my way, including
you. Barry's out of the equation, if he was ever in it. The
question is what does Tiffany want? What will it take to
make *her* happy?

TIFFANY: I want a man in my bed, that's what I want. The one
I had before.

ANNIE: Maybe you'll never get that back.

TIFFANY: I won't, I know it. Like I'll never get those tits back.

She looks at the photo.

ANNIE: But you could.

TIFFANY: These things?

She indicates her breasts –

Like spaniel's ears now. After the kid.

ANNIE: But I think I see *Protest Hero*'s *Bombshell Wife*. I think I
see – I'm sure I do – a photo spread that would give us the
chance to make it up to you for turning those photos down
all those years ago. That's the offer. Naturally there would
be a financial consideration that would be nothing to do
with making sure you kept your mouth shut. Are we on the
same wavelength?

The cautious TIFFANY backs away again –

TIFFANY: That were then, love – (*The photo.*) This is now –

ANNIE: You still have it.

TIFFANY: I were in Tesco's five years back, there was this
bloody great crash. I thought somebody had tipped a
pile of baked bean tins over but it were just me arse had
dropped and hit the floor.

ANNIE: It wouldn't be your Uncle in the spare room this
time. It would be the same photographer who takes the
dogs from the *Big Brother* house and makes them look like
supermodels.

TIFFANY: There's ten years of chips and Mars Bars between
me and her.

ANNIE: With the right photographer –

TIFFANY: You'd need a bleeding miracle worker. Give Jesus
the camera.

ANNIE: But we can work miracles. We do it every day. We'd take some of that – (*The photo.*) – and some new ones and with a little bit of digital magic –

TIFFANY: I let myself go. It's too bloody hard when your fella's away nine months, a year, you're on your jack –

ANNIE: Tiffany – please – do you think Angelina Jolie actually looks like that? In real life? Could anybody? We touch up photos all the time. We add a little bit here, take a little away there, smooth this out, remove a pimple, cover up a blemish, whiten teeth, make eyes bluer, hair roots lighter, turn an A cup into a D and a D into a F –

TIFFANY: But where would *I* be?

ANNIE: You'd still be there.

TIFFANY: Where?

ANNIE: Did you put make-up on today? Yes? Did it make *you* disappear?

TIFFANY: It's not the same.

ANNIE: Think of this as digital make-up.

TIFFANY: It wouldn't be *me.*

ANNIE: But it would be how you'd *want* to be. How your Uncle saw you. How Barry probably sees you – like you were when you first met.

TIFFANY: It'd be a lie.

ANNIE: Given what you've been up to I'd stay clear of that word, I really would. How many Tiffanys are there already? The one when she wakes up in the morning with a face like a bent welly – (*Hastily.*) – if what happens to me overnight is anything to go by – the Tiffany who puts a bit of foundation on to face the day – the Tiffany who goes the whole hog when it's Girl's Night Out and maybe, in the back of your mind, I don't care who you are, married or not, there's the chance of hooking a fella –

TIFFANY: I've not been wi' no one while he's been gone. Wore out the batteries on my Spinster's Friend, if you get my drift.

She makes an electrical buzzing sound –

Bzzz bzzz bzzz.

ANNIE: But you made sure you looked your best when he came home, didn't you? And you stayed *you.*

As she sees TIFFANY hesitate –

Where's *real* now? When you say *this is the truth about something,* aren't you just saying it's the truth now, this minute? You're her – (*The photo.*) – and you're her – and a whole lot of other Tiffany's and maybe the only way to get to a deeper truth about them is some kind of collage. Do you know what a collage is?

TIFFANY: A posh word for a university?

ANNIE: It's a piece of this reality and that reality added together to make a deeper reality. That's what the photo you sold us is – a way of getting at a fundamental truth.

TIFFANY: Even though it's a fake? You say?

ANNIE: In an odd way, believe it or not, *because* it's a fake. Because it's not just reportage but something shaped by a maker's hand. A work of art. You might not have intended it to be that but that's what it is. And I mean that –

She's deadly serious –

That's not bullshit.

TIFFANY: You could have fooled me.

ANNIE: It's like your Uncle, whatever was in his head when he got you to take your clothes off – he ended up with something that was more than a naked girl. He found a deeper truth about you.

TIFFANY: I don't know – he were a bit funny my Uncle Jack, you know. Did six months, later, for boring holes in the Scout Hut changing room wall, they found him with his St Michaels round his ankles holding his willy in his hand in a sock. But maybe that's those artistic types for you...

The lights fade on TIFFANY as she exits with ANNIE as a puzzled KENNEDY enters with MITCH, both in uniform.

KENNEDY: It is nice to see you again, my goodness, chat about old times and that, memories we share and so on but just what are you doing here? I would have thought I'd have been the last person you'd want to have anything to do with. And what is this about a statement? What statement? Barry has a problem. The newspaper has a problem. We do not have a problem. We are in the clear. You are in the clear. You took part in a bit of ill-advised horseplay, that's all. How were you to know somebody else would try to make a bob or two off it? Savage amusement, eh? Egg on a lot of faces but not ours. Not yours. Hell of a result. Very nice. All in the past now, water under the and so on. So what are you doing here? To what do I owe the?

MITCH: A statement –

KENNEDY: Yes?

MITCH: I want to make a statement.

KENNEDY: I think you might have lost the plot here, soldier. Follow this, can you? It's all cleared up. The photo was a fake. As in not real. As in con job. I know they're putting a bit of spin on it, make it some kind of protest which you can quote me is also as fake as the boobs on his missus with her kit off on pages three, four and five – but we're done. And there's the door.

MITCH doesn't move as on the screen we see the image of the naked body again.

MITCH: That photo, right? That's what we're talking about?

KENNEDY: Bingo.

MITCH: It's just, like, when you say it's a fake –

KENNEDY: Yes?

MITCH: Doesn't that depend on what you mean by fake?

KENNEDY: There are no Afghani prisoners being abused on there. There are no Afghanis at all, in fact. *Pas de* gentlemen from Afghanistan. Zero. Not there. Absent on parade.

MITCH: I see that – but it don't make it a fake. I mean a fake is making it look like summat happened that didn't, right? Well what about making it look like summat happened when it did?

KENNEDY: You've – not for the first time – lost me.

MITCH: There's things that didn't happen, only you're saying they did but there's things that did happen that didn't look as if they did, not unless you made them look like they did.

KENNEDY: I'm still having trouble keeping my eye on the ball.

MITCH tries again to be helpful –

MITCH: If summat did happen only nobody knows about it it's different from it not happening and saying it did and knowing it didn't – but it did. I mean, if it did.

KENNEDY: If what did?

MITCH: Happen.

An exasperated KENNEDY indicates the door –

KENNEDY: You're aware of the correct operation of the door handle, are you? Let's just call it a day here and now. I have to be on a plane to Osnabrück at five. Rape complaint. NAAFI cleaner.

MITCH: *Summat happened.*

KENNEDY: No it didn't.

MITCH: But it did.

KENNEDY: No.

MITCH: I were there. But not *there* –

He's indicating the screen again –

I mean, not there, there. I tried to tell you this before. I tried to get it across but you didn't want to listen. Well you have to listen now, all right? I get to say what I have to say. What needs saying. I'm making a statement.

KENNEDY: There's nothing to make a statement about.

MITCH: Yes there is. Would you listen? Would you just listen? Listen, just listen to me.

He indicates the photo on the screen –

What's it showing, eh, that's the question, in't it? What's on there that isn't on there? What isn't on there that should be? I want to get it off my chest, like. It's time I did that. What's in the photo happened, see. For real. A couple of months before.

KENNEDY: Oh.

MITCH: Are you with me?

KENNEDY: Oh shit.

MITCH: Now do you see?

KENNEDY: I hope not.

MITCH: What I'm trying to say is –

KENNEDY: I don't know if I'm the person to hear this –

MITCH: You said have a think about it, come back and see you –

KENNEDY: The door's there. Nobody's heard any of this. Consider.

MITCH: I have.

KENNEDY hesitates, then picks up her pen –

KENNEDY: We're talking about Afghanistan?

MITCH: Yes.

KENNEDY: You want to talk to me about an incident that occurred there which has similarities to the events depicted in that photo?

MITCH: Right.

KENNEDY: Involving similar mistreatment of prisoners?

MITCH: Right.

KENNEDY: Then I think I ought to warn you that you don't have to say anything to me but anything you do say –

He ignores her –

MITCH: Couldn't get it out of my mind. That night. It were wrong, I knew that. But I got dragged into it. It were always, like, I were the one on the outside, hanging back. They thought I were soft, like. Always on at me. Taking the Mick.

KENNEDY: You're aware that you're making this statement under caution?

He still ignores her –

MITCH: Used to have this game, *Boiler Nights*, didn't we? You'd have to pick up the ugliest bird in the club, wait until she went to the khazi and then have a crap in her handbag. I thought that were a rotten thing to do. But you have to go along, don't you? I mean, these are the blokes going to be looking out for you, when you're up the sharp end, like –

KENNEDY tries to get him back on track –

KENNEDY: The photo –

MITCH: Funny thing were, I liked it out there. You might say it's the Middle bloody Ages but I liked the way of life, everybody on the street, how busy it all were; the old fellas up the mosque calling for prayers and that. I liked the people. Some of them hated our guts and didn't try to hide it but the others –? Well we weren't patrolling like the Yanks, behind armour, looking like Robo man, we was in the streets, like, in the market, yomping it, getting to know them. Yeah. I liked it out there. I liked Iraq, too. I could have done without them chucking bombs at us but now and again you went –*it's interesting, this is, it's really interesting.*

KENNEDY: The photo –?

MITCH: (*Doggedly.*) There were this religious festival going on one place; hundreds, thousands of them all in white, heading for the mosque; everybody dressed the same; little kiddies and all. I never saw owt like it. It were like they all knew where they belonged. This was it, right? Where they was meant to be; there weren't any question about it; they had the answer. You know what I mean, *the answer*? Summat that would take you in; give you back; you just had to say yes. I mean a big yes. Not a half-hearted one. You'd have to go the whole way, all the way, buy everything about it. Had to keep me mouth shut about that in front of the lads, of course. They didn't see it like that at all. So I had to join in, like, that night. When Baz and them started messing around with the prisoner. I mean, how would it look if I were the only one not?

KENNEDY: Joining in with the kind of treatment we can see there?

She indicates the photo –

The abuse? Humiliation?

MITCH: It were like Boiler Night only wi'out the tarts.

KENNEDY: But somebody got hurt?

MITCH: Not hurt, no. Slapped around a bit, maybe but that were all. It were just a lark.

KENNEDY: Such a good one that you all decided to make a record of it when you got back? That could be sold to the papers? To make some money?

MITCH: There you go again. I'd no idea about that. When I saw it in the paper I said *bloody hell. That was just like it was.* And then you had me in and had a go but I couldn't get my head around it, that's all I was trying to do, get my head around it but you had all these questions and I'm going *They must know,* I mean *How could they not know,* I mean, Barry, I ask you, *Barry,* they must have his number so why are they doing my head in, me?

On the screen appears a photo of an Afghani man –

KENNEDY: Do you recognise him?

MITCH: I don't –

KENNEDY: Was he the prisoner abused that night?

MITCH: He could have been.

KENNEDY: You can't say for sure?

MITCH: It's hard to –

KENNEDY: If I told you he had a brother who was picked up at the same time and a special point was made of having the two of them together?

MITCH: I were just – it were mainly Paddy and Dave, like – it were them and Baz but they're dead, aren't they? They both bought it out there.

KENNEDY: So it's just your word against Baz's word?

MITCH: (*Stubborn.*) I'm saying how it was. That I can't get it out of my mind. Not now I'm back. I'm there, all the time, in me head. Waiting for somebody to throw a rock, for a bomb to go off beside the road, a mortar round to come in. But mainly I'm there that night. Joining in.

He looks troubled –

When somebody's shooting at you, that's one thing, right? That's about *them.* But when you've got them on the floor, at your feet, and you're putting them through that, it's about *you* so I have to put this right, what I did out there.

KENNEDY slides pen and paper across the desk towards him. He takes the pen, hesitates, the starts to write slowly and deliberately and the lights fade on him and KENNEDY, who exits. ANNIE enters reads from MITCH's statement –

ANNIE: *Couldn't get it out of my mind. That night. It were wrong, I knew that. But I got dragged into it. It were always, like, I were the one on the outside, hanging back. They thought I were soft, like. Always on at me. Taking the Mick. Used to have this game, Boiler Nights, didn't we? You'd have to pick up the ugliest bird in the club, wait until she went to the khazi and then have a crap in her handbag. I thought that were a rotten thing to do. But you*

have to go along, don't you? I mean, these are the blokes going to
be looking out for you, when you're up the sharp end, like –

The lights rise on a shaken KYLE –

KYLE: Let me see if I have this straight. We ran with a photo
that turned out to be put-up job and to get our bollocks off
the barbed wire we made Barry a hero and ran a special
on his missus' knockers to keep them quiet but now it
turns out that while the photo of the abuse is still a fake
it's not quite such a fake, it's more what you might call
a reconstruction of an actual event painting Barry, who
we've just turned into a hero with a very shaggable wife, all
things considering, as a potential war criminal? Are those
the main headings?

ANNIE: I'm wondering if it isn't too late to go back to being
innocent victims of a con-man and his wife?

KYLE: Now that we've made him *Hero's Afghan Nightmare –*
Underdog Fights Back? Glamour Past Of Warrior Wife – Saucy
Mum Bares All For The Boys?

Pissed, he stares up at a photo of BARRY on the screen in
uniform –

It's over. We're done for. (*Bitterly.*) You know what the
British soldier is? The scum of the earth. Wellington
had his number. And Kipling. Thank God, between you
and me, for a war every few years when we can ship his
sneakered, shell-suited, lager-lout, pimpled arse abroad,
where he can play merry hell with the Wogs, the Paddies
and the Arabs instead of infesting our High Streets at
closing time with his drunken mates and with any luck
he'll get himself killed in some foreign field that will be
forever England instead of coming back and sticking his
unwashed prick in some ugly cow from a housing estate
like good old Tiffany and infecting the world with yet
more of his kind. We've been shipping Barry and his like

abroad for two hundred years; taking his bad breath, smelly feet, gonorrhoea and stupidity with him; the ugliest member of the ugliest race in Europe; giving him just enough education to believe he's superior to everyone else on earth and a contempt for the lesser breeds he's going to be living among or fighting. Now, God help us all, good old Barry is engaged on our behalf in a battle for the world; the men of the desert versus the men of the cities; the West versus militant Islam; engaged in a duel that has been going on for fifteen hundred years; a quarrel that has changed the face of Europe time after time; he's the heir to El Cid and the *reconquista*; the knights who stopped the Turks at the gates of Vienna; who saved Europe for Christianity and secular democracy and if you ask him what the experience was like he'd say 'it were bloody hot'. He's indestructible. When we blow ourselves up the only things left on earth will be the cockroach and him and his scheming missus and you and me had best be checking to see if the *Bridlington Fish Frier's Weekly* has anything for us because we are right royally fucked –

The lights fade on them and they exit. MITCH stands to face TIFFANY and BARRY as they enter –

MITCH: (*To BARRY.*) I wanted no part of it, you know that. That night. And I kept me mouth shut when they came asking. But it were wrong. You know it were wrong.

TIFFANY: I'll tell you what were wrong, mate. The Army buggering him around for the money they owed him. *Have you got this form, have you got that form? Date of injury? Date of discharge?* If he'd fallen off a roof trying to break into somebody's house they'd have treated him better.

BARRY: A lot of stuff happened out there. Bad stuff. But it don't mean nowt.

TIFFANY: (*To MITCH*). You couldn't keep your spastic mouth shut?

MITCH: You have to put things right. You know you have to.

TIFFANY: He don't know nowt. He wasn't there. He doesn't know what you're talking about. You're making it up. Nowt happened. Except in your spastic head. Which you're trying to put into his, I don't know why, when half the time he don't know which way is up anyway, the state he's in.

MITCH: Why would I make it up?

TIFFANY: Haven't a clue. Don't know the first thing about you. You've got your own reasons for saying it but I think you might want to leave us out of it, I really do. Whatever your game is. And who's going to back you up, anyway?

MITCH: Dave and Paddy were there.

TIFFANY: Well they ain't now, are they? They're in a box. So it's just your word, in't it?

MITCH turns to look at her with a kind of admiration –

MITCH: Saw you in the paper. Smashing. You looked – bloody hell, I *mean*.

TIFFANY: Is it money? Is that what you want? Here –

She pulls a handful of banknotes out of her handbag –

Take it. Have it.

MITCH: I don't want –

TIFFANY: Is that what it is? Make a few bob, take your statement back, it never happened?

MITCH: It happened.

TIFFANY: Here's a thing, blackmail your mates –

She indicates BARRY –

Somebody who don't know the day of the week half the time; take advantage like that –

MITCH: *It happened.*

TIFFANY: Look at him –

She indicates BARRY, slumped on his crutches –

I mean *look at him.*

As MITCH looks at BARRY –

Put summat right? You want to put summat right? How about putting him right? Take more than a bloody *statement,* wouldn't it?

She throws the money at him and the lights fade on BARRY and MITCH who exit as KENNEDY enters. TIFFANY goes on the attack at once –

It don't mean owt and you know it. It's his word against Barry's that it ever happened.

KENNEDY: Why would he lie?

TIFFANY: Ask him.

KENNEDY: I have. I'm sure he's telling the truth. I have his statement.

TIFFANY: But that's all you've got, in't it?

KENNEDY: There's the photo.

TIFFANY: It's a fake, that is. You want to read the papers, you do.

On the screen appear headlines reading 'Hero Vet Reveals Secret Behind That Photo. One Man's Brave Protest.'

KENNEDY: I saw that attempt to spin the story, yes –

TIFFANY: You saw how much?

She thrusts out the tape recorder again, into KENNEDY's face –

You want to be careful what you're saying, mate, that's libel that is. Even if you are in a bloody Boy Scouts' uniform.

KENNEDY: But it isn't such a fake, is it? The photo?

TIFFANY: You want to make your mind up, you do. Is it or in't it?

KENNEDY: Maybe it's both.

TIFFANY: How could that be then?

KENNEDY: Maybe it's not one thing or the other. Or maybe it's both at the same time. The way I am, you might say, a soldier in this – Boy Scout's uniform – but a lawyer, too.

TIFFANY: You trying to do my head in?

KENNEDY: I think you're far too smart for that. You've run rings around a national newspaper.

TIFFANY: Can you speak up?

She thrusts the tape recorder in KENNEDY's face again.

Our Barry in't in the army any more, is he? So you can't touch him.

KENNEDY: We need his help in investigating these allegations.

TIFFANY: How far do you think you'll get, Sherlock? There's no other witnesses, are there? Paddy and Dave? Six feet under, aren't they? I should think you're well stuffed, love.

KENNEDY: We'll see about that.

TIFFANY: Do you have to be a lesbian to join the army or will they let you convert after? You don't look like a dyke but you never can tell, can you? There were an aunt of mine who looked like butter wouldn't melt in her mouth turned out to be a biker at the weekends, muff diving in leather all over the shop which we only found out about when she went under a lorry on the M6 carrying a load of French fries for McDonalds and nobody'd believe it until her girlfriend turned up at the funeral on a Harley Davidson with her name tattooed on her left tit.

She indicates the door –

Lift's out of order again, when you leave. You'll have to take the stairs. You want to be careful going down them, pet – the lights are out. Somebody give you a shove, you could really get messed up, lie there for hours, you could. God knows what'd happen to you then, some of the buggers around here. You'd be lucky to get out wi' your knickers in your hand. Khaki, are they?

KENNEDY stands her ground –

KENNEDY: I'm asking again to see your husband.

TIFFANY: See, the thing about being out of the army is you've got rights. You can choose. It's like, it used to be *Edgewater – get your arse to Iraq and Afghanistan so you can get your bollocks shot off* but it ain't like that no more, is it? You've got nowt if he don't make a statement and he ain't making one.

As if genuinely interested in the answer again –

So were you just too thick to get a proper job as a lawyer? Is that why you had to go in the army? Nobody else'd have you?

Beat –

He's having a bad day. You know what a bad day is? It's when he's got so many pills inside him he's a zombie. Only I still have to watch it because anything sets him off. Like I can't even let Brittany near him because he might throw her off the balcony of the flat. Or like this –

She tugs her blouse open to show a livid yellow and purple bruise –

– like he did three days ago. That's what a bad day is. Since he got back. Since he got away from you. After what you did to him. So I don't think you'll be talking to him, no. I don't think that's a good idea at all. It ain't going to happen. So where does that leave you, eh?

The lights fade on KENNEDY and TIFFANY who exit as KYLE enters with ANNIE. BARRY enters, uncertain, borderline hostile –

BARRY: She's out. Has to work two jobs now. It's just me and the baby.

KYLE: It's you we need to talk to.

BARRY: Her. You talk to *her*.

Uneasy, he heads away but KYLE blocks him –

KYLE: Mitch says –

BARRY: I know what he says.

KYLE: Your good mate says –

BARRY: He ain't no mate of mine. He never were.

ANNIE: We want to stand by you, Barry. The paper wants to stand by you. We did right by you, didn't we? By both of you? Made you out to be some kind of hero? Kept our word and ran those pictures of Tiffany –?

On the screen we see the new, digitally enhanced photos of TIFFANY –

KYLE: (*Hastily.*) The two things of course having nothing to do with each other.

BARRY: (*Grudging.*) They came out good, yeah.

ANNIE: They did, didn't they? She'd be feeling good about herself, I should think. You'd be happy that she's happy. But now we have this other thing, don't we?

BARRY: Nowt to do wi' me what Mitch says.

KYLE: He's given a statement. On oath.

BARRY: I can't see it's owt to do wi' me, I really can't.

He looks up at the photos of TIFFANY –

Funny but – I did always see her like that. She always were summat special. Just needed somebody bringing it out.

KYLE: You're one thing or the other. You're either a hero or you're the villain Mitch's testimony makes you out to be. We know what the paper wants you to be. But we need you to level with us. There's nothing that can't be fixed –

He indicates the photos of TIFFANY –

That's proof of that, right? How much you can make things come out how you want them? If you want them badly enough? If you're smart? But we have to start off on the same foot. We have to know there won't be any other little surprises.

BARRY: You've been fair to me. More than fair. You think I wouldn't tell you? If there were?

ANNIE: The world would be a wonderful place if we could just look into each other's big blue eyes and accept what we're being told. Unfortunately –

BARRY: I'm being straight wi' you. That's God's truth, that is. Mitch ain't got owt.

ANNIE: But at the moment it's your word against his. And his is on a very official looking sheet of paper with blood-curdling threats printed at the top against anybody telling fibs.

KYLE: You, on the other hand, are a con man.

BARRY: You what?

KYLE: That's how it would look, if it ever came out, the game you and Tiffany have been playing.

ANNIE: But we're here to make sure that doesn't happen. We need heroes. Real heroes. Haven't got that many these days, have we? Have to make them up out of whatever odds and ends we have. Soap stars. One-hit-wonders on their way in or out of rehab. Actors whose names you vaguely remember whose films you never saw but you might rent having seen them on *You Tube* being stretchered out of their flat after they OD'd. You're the best we've got. You're a warrior and even what Tiffany's done fits the story.

BARRY: You talked her into getting her nips out, that's all.

ANNIE: The Amazons bared their breasts when they went into battle. Boadicea did the same. Or I think she did.

BARRY: Who?

ANNIE: Early feminist icon. Big wheels with spikes sticking out. The point is you fought back and Tiffany fought back in the only way she could. You're a great story – wounded hero, beautiful young wife –young*ish* –

KYLE: He's black and angry. We know his sort. We have his number. There's the Good Black, the cool black – soccer star, rapper, celebrity chef. There's the Bad Black. Morose bugger, brooding on the history of his race, always looking for a way to get back at The Man. Whoever The Man is at any one time. There's no contest. We could really do him over. But we have to know we can go with you. Which means, in general, no more *holy fuck* moments where you and your missus are concerned.

He spreads him arms wide and ANNIE does the same –

No tape recorder. Just you and us.

BARRY: I'm trying to get me head round this, I really am. Mitch is saying somebody did what's on the photo to one of the A-rabs?

ANNIE: Yes.

BARRY: And they've got the A-rab it were done to?

ANNIE: And he's made a statement.

BARRY: He can't have. Because it weren't owt to do wi' him.

KYLE: We know it's him.

BARRY: No you don't.

KYLE: The Army interviewed him.

BARRY: No it didn't.

ANNIE takes out another sheet of paper, reads –

ANNIE: *First they put the dogs on me. They hit me here and here. Then they said they would do sex with me. They would make me do sex with men. Then one of them said I would do sex with the dog first. I beg them not to take my clothes off but they say take everything off or you will be bitten by the dog again.*

BARRY: What's he saying that for?

KYLE: Because it happened to him.

BARRY: He couldn't have done.

KYLE: He did. She just read it out to you.

BARRY: No he didn't. Not the fella the photo were about. He didn't give nobody no statement, I guarantee that.

KYLE: Mitch –

BARRY: I don't care what *Mitch.*

KYLE: The Army –

BARRY: I don't care what *the Army*.

KYLE: Is everybody lying but you?

BARRY: I'm not saying he's lying –

KYLE: You just did.

BARRY: I never.

ANNIE sees that KYLE is about to lose control, steps in –

ANNIE: Let's make sure we're all talking about the same thing, shall we? We are talking about the photo in your cell phone?

BARRY: Yes.

ANNIE: The photo you took?

BARRY: No.

KYLE: No?

BARRY: I never said I took it.

ANNIE: I have you on tape saying it.

BARRY: You don't.

KYLE: She does.

BARRY: She doesn't.

KYLE: Yes she does.

BARRY: No she doesn't.

The lighting state changes as ANNIE and BARRY reprise the initial interview again –

BARRY: *You could say it were just a lark.*

ANNIE: *A lark?*

BARRY: *It were just a fragment of fun.*

ANNIE: *You really want me to write that?*

BARRY: *I don't care what you write, pet, I'm just telling you. It looks a lot worse than it were.*

ANNIE: *Our readers may find that hard to believe.*

BARRY: *They can believe what they like, pet.*

ANNIE: *You did take that photo, though?*

BARRY: *I might have done.*

ANNIE: *But you're saying you didn't have any responsibility for what it shows?*

BARRY: *Am I?*

ANNIE: *You were just the finger on the button?*

BARRY: *Was I?*

ANNIE: *Even so, you were involved.*

BARRY: *How's that, then?*

They reprise the first of the crucial phrases on the recording –

ANNIE: *You did take that photo, though?*

BARRY: *I might have done.*

ANNIE: *You did take that photo, though?*

BARRY: *I might have done.*

They reprise the second one –

ANNIE: *You were just the finger on the button?*

BARRY: *Was I?*

ANNIE: *You were just the finger on the button?*

BARRY: *Was I?*

KYLE reacts, realising that BARRY is telling him the exact truth about what he admitted and what he didn't admit.

KYLE: Jesus –

ANNIE: Bloody hell –

KYLE: Oh my God –

ANNIE: I don't, do I? Have him saying it?

BARRY: What I told you. You don't.

ANNIE: But if you didn't take it –

KYLE: Who took it? Who took the bloody thing?

BARRY: Dave took it on his mobile, right and sent it to my mobile, right? I were going to delete it but Tiffs sees it and says there might be a couple of bob in, right? I were having a bad go, see. They knew that. That's why they sent it. It were like *–we had some good fucking times, didn't we? Keep your pecker up.* They were my mates, see. They knew what I were going through. They send me the photo and two days after, they bought it. Copped a suicide bomber, woman with a kilo of high explosive in her burkha; when they found their heads the kiddies were playing football wi' them a hundred yards away. And that were funny, that were. Dave could never stand the game.

KYLE: I think –

He looks as if he's run out of steam –

That puts a whole new –

Helplessly, he turns to ANNIE –

We'd better –

His shoulders go down –

We'll have a think about this –

ANNIE is about to leave with him when a thought strikes her –

ANNIE: Wait –

KYLE: Let's go.

ANNIE: No wait. Wait. He just said something, something that doesn't –

KYLE: I wouldn't like to have this thing fucked up any more than it already is –

ANNIE: No, wait. *Wait.*

She's searching her memory, desperate to figure something out, turns to BARRY –

You said *No he didn't. Not the fella the photo were about.*

BARRY: Did I? I don't know about that. You're doing my head in, you are.

ANNIE: *No he didn't. Not the fella the photo were about.*

KYLE isn't following this –

KYLE: He said that, yes but –?

ANNIE: How many people are we talking about here? If it's not *the fella the photo were about* then –

She turns to BARRY again –

Were there two men? More than two? There were certainly more than one, right?

BARRY: I thought you was going –

ANNIE: (*Persistent.*) Was that it? Is that why you can be so certain? That it wasn't that one?

BARRY: No I think you'd really better go.

ANNIE: One, say, who was a little fuzzy on dates who the Army interviewed, who gave this statement –

BARRY: I think you better had.

ANNIE: So who was the other? What happened to him?

BARRY: You better had go.

ANNIE turns to KYLE, certain that she's on the verge of something big but uncertain what it is –

ANNIE: You see? *Not the fella the photo were about.* In which case there had to be somebody else but why would he be so certain he wouldn't give a statement?

Suddenly KYLE gets it –

KYLE: There'd be one reason, wouldn't there? One very good one.

A fraction after him, ANNIE gets it –

ANNIE: No –

KYLE: No?

He turns to BARRY –

Just what have you told her?

BARRY: I've told her nowt. *Nowt.*

KYLE: What have you just said?

BARRY looks agitated –

BARRY: You can stuff those photos. Stuff them up your arse. Do what you fucking like wi' them. I've had it wi' the whole shoot, I have.

KYLE's voice is shaking as he tries to lock everything down –

KYLE: Two men. One reason why one of them didn't give that statement. (*To ANNIE.*) Good. Bloody good. You might not be going to Bridlington after all. (*Back to BARRY.*) He'd never be in a position to give a statement? Was that it?

ANNIE: Was that it, Barry? Is that what it was?

KYLE: Is that what you're trying to tell us?

ANNIE: Maybe it's something you've not even told Tiffany – but you can tell us –

She tries to keep her voice level –

I can't ask you to trust us because we're not here as us. We're here as the paper. What we do with anything you tell us is out of our hands. But we're not the army and we're not the police. People tell us all sorts of things that they need to get off their chests. It helps them. It helps them let go of things. You might find it helps you.

BARRY: Tiffs, see – she don't – there are things she knows and things she –

ANNIE: You've protected her. We get it. Whatever you tell us we'll make sure she's still protected.

BARRY: Nobody'll ever be able to prove nowt. Not now.

ANNIE: But Dave and Paddy were reminding you of something that happened. That night. And Mitch knows some of it –

Before he can angrily respond –

– or he thinks he does. But he doesn't know it all, does he?

KYLE: What's the bit he doesn't know?

ANNIE gestures to him to back off – she's going to deal with BARRY now –

ANNIE: What would be the reason he'd think he knows?

BARRY: He were there.

ANNIE: Right.

BARRY: He were there that night.

ANNIE: Right.

BARRY: But he fucked off. After a bit. The night we was –

ANNIE: The night the photo refers to?

BARRY: The night we done the A-rab.

KYLE reacts but again ANNIE indicates he should back off, leave this to her –

ANNIE: That statement of his –

BARRY: His heart weren't really in it. He's a bit of a poof, I always reckoned.

ANNIE: So if he fucked off, that means he was there at the beginning?

BARRY: Yes.

ANNIE: Of what? The beginning of what?

BARRY: We'd had a bad few days. Lost two fellas. Been told we was going to be staying on an extra month. Then the MPs brought in this fella who'd been working in the kitchens, like, only they reckoned he'd been passing on information to the Taliban, intelligence, which was why the two fellas had bought it, down to him. Normally he'd have been all squared away in secure housing but they'd dropped a mortar on it so he were at the end of the corridor, temporary, while they sorted his paperwork out. Then Paddy sees the MPs have fucked off to run somebody else in and the coast is clear, right, to get stuck in.

ANNIE: (*Carefully.*) Stuck in? What exactly –

BARRY: We'd been getting some stick from Two Para about
not getting a grip on the sector, see, not making sure
everybody knew we was boss. You don't like to be called
soft, do you, especially when it's the Afghans you're
dealing with, right tough buggers, even the kiddies'd cut
your throat soon as look at you.

*The light fades on KYLE, isolates BARRY and ANNIE as she gently
but expertly questions him –*

ANNIE: Getting back to that night – in the barracks –

BARRY: So here's a chance, right, to show we can do the
business good as anyone; get the word out, don't mess wi'
us. He were a right lippy cunt, this one, picked up a bit of
the lingo somewhere which made it all the worse. Specially
wi' Dave. He didn't like non-white people talking English,
for some reason it drove him up the wall so he piles in and
Paddy has some and I had a bit and so does Mitch, even,
though he's soft as shite and the fella's still giving it wi' the
verbal even though his teeth are decorating the fucking
room b'now and then it getsa bit heavy.

ANNIE: Heavy?

BARRY: I mean, heavy. Which is when Mitch piles out, picks
up his petticoats and fucks on off and now it's who's going
to crack first. The A-rab or him. Are we going all the
way? If we have to? Now me, see, I never thought it were
meant to be owt but a bit of fun but Dave and Paddy,
they were right devils they were, always egging each other
on. Smashing lads but they was always trying to – I don't
know – enough were never enough. Especially when the
question's being put, see – *how far do we take this?*

ANNIE: How far did it go? Can you tell me?

BARRY: I'm not saying I'm blameless because I might have lost it a bit m'self because all I want the fella to do is just shut the fuck up and admit he's had his beating and give over. Instead of which he's still looking game so I give him one more thump and then another and not even that does the trick and why doesn't the silly bugger just give it up, that's what's really pissing me off, that he's not doing himself no favours, it's him that's keeping this going now, we want to jack it in, call it a night but the silly sod just won't lie there and keep his gob shut. What's left of it after Paddy measured it wi' his boot. Well anyway up, after a bit events take their inevitable course, you might say, and the fella makes this gurgling noise which made Dave go a bit madder, even, which I agree there's no call for but we was all nuts by this time, barking mad the lot of us, what a fucking night when we could have been watching a video with the other lads.

ANNIE: But instead you'd –

BARRY: And by the time we pulled him off the fella ain't breathing.

ANNIE: He wasn't –

BARRY: What I said.

ANNIE tries not to react but her voice is shaky –

ANNIE: There's Dave and Paddy and you and there's a body –

BARRY: What I said.

ANNIE: Mitch has gone, he doesn't know any of this and there's a body and what then? You have to get rid of the body?

BARRY: (*Sarcastic.*) No, we're just going to leave it lying there, brighten the place up a bit. We had a bit of luck, we was in this old provincial governor's compound or summat wi' a water tank out the back so we had him down there. Next day Mitch is asking what happened but the three of us said nowt. We didn't know if we could trust the black bugger, which in the event, the way things went – (*Shrug.*) – the MPs weren't too fucking happy, come back and find him gone but we'd had a chance, clean the place up, get a story straight. So that's that, in't it? That's why Mitch is talking through his hat. He weren't here when we done the bugger.

The lights fade on ANNIE, leaving BARRY lit by himself –

I knew it'd come to this. I knew somebody'd figure it out. You know when things just keep coming at you? Some bugger wants this and some bugger wants that and you can't think straight and anything you do you're just digging yourself deeper into it, making more trouble for yourself but you can't do nowt? That's what I miss about the army, about the life. It were simple. *Do this, do that, get your arse over there, come back here, hold this, let go of that, yes sarge, no sarge, three bags full sarge* but you knew where you where, what was expected. Even at the sharp end you had that to fall back on. *Eyes wide, sniper, double-up, fall back, grab your pack, gun and run, hit the dirt.* It were all laid out, like your kit. *This goes here, that goes there and bob's your uncle.* Civvy Street, bloody Civvy Street? I don't understand it, straight up, I don't. Can't get it into me head.

A rueful grin –

I knew some bugger'd put two and two together. About that dead Arab. In the end. Took their time though, didn't they? They're all talk, I reckon. When you get down to it they're thick as two planks. Thick as a Welshman's cock.

He tucks one of the crutches under his arm, takes out a small firearm –

Me dad brought this home from the Falklands. Beretta. Semi auto. Thirteen round clip. Had it off an Argie at Goose Green –

He puts the barrel into his mouth and as he fires the lights go out on him and the screen turns red. We snap to black and

End.